from the stillness within

a poetry collection

katelyn millett

from the stillness within

Portions of the text were previously published in another format on the author's social media.
Original version of "internal peace" can be found on the website *Words to Sit With*

Library of Congress Control Number: 2025906857

First edition
ISBN 979-8-218-57444-4
Printed in the United States of America

for my sisters, Rachel and Jenna,
you are reflections of the better parts of me

contents

nature does not hurry,
yet everything is accomplished.

Lao Tzu

CHAPTER ONE:

wanderer

first page

hello, dear friend.
i welcome you,
pen in hand,
and all of the opportunities
in your blank pages.

the warm embrace,
the fresh starts,
the confirmations.

expressions, questions, hopes,
dreams, inner-conflicts, mantras,
intentions
and reflections.

a mixed symphony
of an inner world
brought to life on paper.
such a physical thing
found in a world
built on daydreams.

we're all just here
trying to make sense
of it all.

introduction

i was first named katelyn,
but i go by kate.

i was raised religious,
but i questioned my faith.
i feel God outside of books.
i seek for him/her/they/we
in truth that speaks to me,
which lately hasn't been in a church.

i use pen and paint to express my emotions,
to release what's inside.
i write poems of words that fall
from clouds in my mind.
i use paint to spill my thoughts -
the colors of an inner world coming to life.

i have dreams that would be so real
if i only knew how to believe,
really believe,
in the face of time, doubt and fatigue.
these dreams include seeing the world,
giving back to my home,
growing wings to fly
and inspiring change in others
who also forgot they could touch the sky.

i believe in rainbows
and butterflies.
i don't know how
to love everyone yet,
but i do know how to love hard.
it's a crux.
it's a gift.

i'm consistent in that i'm inconsistent.
inconsistent in what i think i desire.
i want to travel.
i want a home.
i want community.
sometimes i want to be alone.

duality - one of the greatest illusions of all.

my spirituality rides the tide.

faith.
a flow of passion and healing
coming in on waves
with an undercurrent strength
i somehow underestimate.

i want to leave my mark on this world.
have i done my part if i don't?

legacy.

i want to leave a legacy,
i need to leave a legacy,
i -
...is this ego or self-fulfilling prophecy?

perspective.

i value questioning who i am.
the core of being.
i'm trying to be here now.

beliefs.
the lenses through which
we interact with the world.
they're made from thoughts,
built on sand
and as fleeting as the wind.
is that what i am?

all i really know
is that i'm here.

i go by kate.
i like to write poetry and paint.
and someday, maybe today,
i'll use my wings to fly.

universal worlds

i write words
gifted by the sweet lips of destiny,
an offering to the here and now,
embracing the oneness
mirrored by the stars
and mapped out in our minds,
constantly re-written
to keep time
with the mysterious lullaby
of the universe
that only God knows.

<u>am i?</u>

am i divinity,
a satin sheet distance away
from touching and feeling
divine truth's breath?

am i a dark mystery,
exploring the depths and the bottom
of the sea?

am i the limbs of a tree,
holding the wisdom of history
beneath my skin?

let go and you will see
the you that longs to be set free.

disillusioned

you think you know me, but you don't.
i don't even know myself.

you're disillusioned and that's okay.

who am i to tell you that you're wrong?
you only see what you want to see.
we all do.

<u>prose</u>

"see me"
becomes an illusion
under assumptions of identity
where the real me, not the ego,
wouldn't ask for that at all.

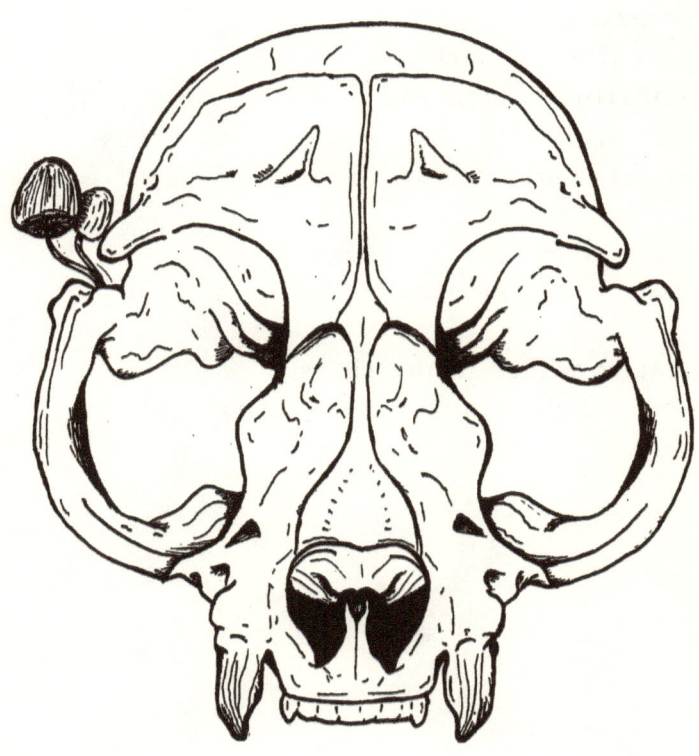

coffee shop

this world both unravels
and pieces me together again.
a back-and-forth game
of cutting and sewing
to form a person that i'll pretend
is me.

awareness of self
and seeking validation -
two mirrors in a standoff.
constant choices
crafted through conditioning.

who are you?
who are you compared to they?

a hamster wheel of questions
answered by paradoxes and duality.

forgotten songs

aren't we always
learning a dance
that the wind is already playing?

keeping time with the stars
that the ghosts of a past life
once lived?

why do i try so hard
to stay ahead of a path
that was already written
before i began?

eye

being someone who seeks after truth
is like mapping the stars
and running in loops
on a playground of questions
that all start with "why",
but look deep enough
and you'll come to the "I".

<u>seeking</u>

in the midst of all that's happening,
and happened
and sure to happen,
i desire more,
yet i fear change.

i want more.
i've always wanted more.
to do more,
to have more.

but, when i finally do more,
i value doing less.

a balance.
too far to one side
and i'm already looking back.

when will i learn
that what i really want
is already here?

<u>daydreaming</u>

cotton candy in the skyline
like a blanket of dreams.
take my hand, it's safe.
there's no falling from here.

close your eyes.
the air is sweeter
when your mind is free to taste
the uncensored.

let go of tomorrow,
of the past, of the present.
illusions bred from sweet lips
and universal shows.

rolling oceans sweep over lands
full of unanswered ghosts.
where's the breath of life
when the only thing seen is smoke?

it's all smoke.
where no one questions,
and no one knows
and no one knows how to question.

there's a scramble for security
when illusions are tested -

nothing holds.
it's an empty showcase wrapped in gold.

there's bliss in the ignorance
of the reality
that there is no true reality.

truth.

let go of uncertainty
and take a dip into infinity.

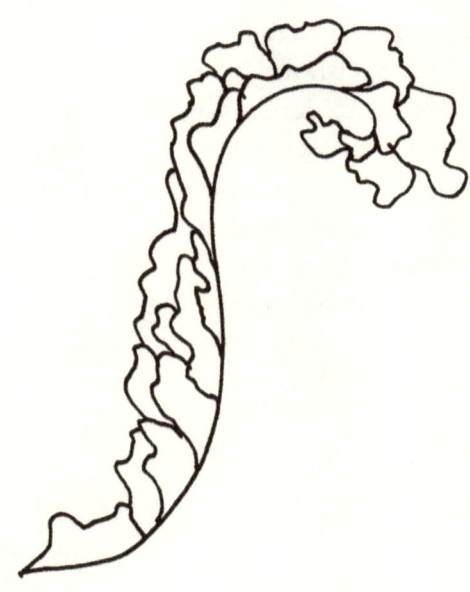

running thoughts

sometimes i wish i could take a picture
of the thoughts running through my mind.
they're always changing.
a river with endless bends,
and i never know what's coming next.
by the time i grasp hold of one idea
or emotion,
it's already changing,
or i forget,
like a flash of lightning
not even my camera can get.
i don't know how to understand myself, then.
endless future ideas
and so many plans.
loose plans, because who knows
who i'll be tomorrow
if i'm already someone new today
from who i was yesterday?
new because who knew?
who knew i'd be new?

<u>blue</u>

blue are my thoughts.
they come and they go
from places deep
and unknown.

but, this is my head, after all.

if this world,
this world full of blue,
is only something
that i thought that i knew,
then is this mind even mine?

what's the truth?

<u>stars I</u>

i want to go to the moon
and see what the stars sing about
when they dance in its light
with the world's dreams in their eyes.

stars II

tell me, dark night, why there's light in your eyes
when the coal is no match for your heart.
why do the shadows hide at your name
but the stars mixed with you create art?

<u>stars III</u>

i tear open my chest to see if it's there,
the heart that they all say i have.
relief floods my eyes when i see what's inside.
a constellation of stars without end.

disconnection

my being in this body
feels crooked and disconnected.

sometimes i feel like i'm living third-person
just thinking,
thinking,
thinking.

listening to the mind without any regard
to the body.

sometimes i treat my body as if it's not even mine.
sometimes the only time i care
is when it's an inconvenience.

it suffers,
and i blame it.

who is "it"?
who is "i"?

this disconnection is seen
from my past,
hemmed in from skewed validations
and not feeling like enough.

this disconnection is part

of a deepening self-awareness.

this re-connection is part
of my healing,
empowerment
and self-love.

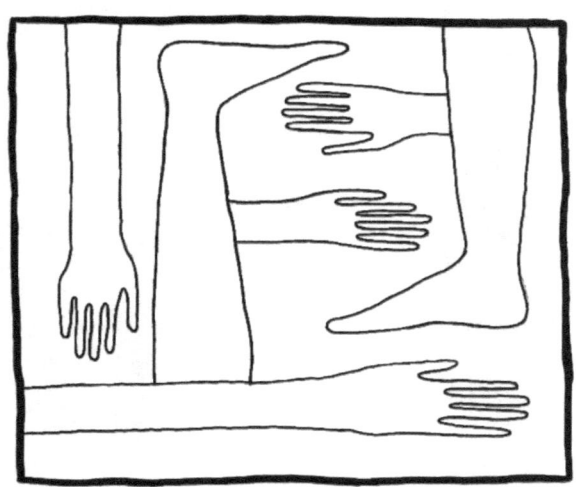

<u>inner guide</u>

i feel so lost,
yet i'm right here.
where is my connection to source?
where is my inner guidance,
my compass and my map?

the outside noise is loud,
still i keep changing the station
instead of turning it off.

my inner voice is quiet.
it arises from the stillness,
sometimes felt,
not heard.

why is it so hard for me
to be still
and just listen?
i feel conflicted.

fractal support

the base of my identity, my family,
feels like a house built on sand.
no consistency
except inconsistency.
something so broken.

but when a cloud breaks,
the sky doesn't grieve.
it's a natural mosaic
of life moving on.
constant change.

nature breaking
is also the beginning
of something new.
death reborn
as its previous form is lost.

a kaleidoscope
stuck on one image.
eyes stuck to one view.
take it away?
infinity anew.

<u>seen</u>

i want to be a good person.
sometimes i fear that i'm not.

i want to help others
feel seen.

sometimes i worry
that all i care about
is how i'm seen by others.

<u>enough</u>

why does my heart sometimes feel
like it's not worthy to be held?

why do i give my power away to others
when it was never
theirs to be had?

why do i desire being told
that i'm loveable
and deserving?

why do i crave the need
to be reminded i'm enough?

when did i forget
that i have always been enough?

contrast

what if people seem to die
so that those still breathing
feel more alive?

<u>cathedral walls</u>

sadness washes over me
like a blanket,
tied down
with invisible fears.
i wear it for comfort,
protected by towering walls
i can barely see over.

this sadness is heavy with grief.
everything hurts.
it is dark, this pride.

i dare scream out,
"who goes there?!"

but no,
it's just me.
suffering is a choice,
so lose the pity.

internal suffering

there is real pain in this world -
war, grief and loss,
just to name a few.
in times like these,
a deep part within
sometimes feels stuck
in a deep, dark place
i otherwise forget was there.

why, then, do i
create my own pain?
internal suffering
caused by "what ifs"
and never ending desires.
focusing on what i want
and on what i don't have.

why do i create more pain
than there needs to be?

darkness

into the darkness,
i search for the light.
hands outstretched.
feet stumble over the unknown.
air is tight.
paranoia sweeps through me.
i become desperate.
"help!"

my breath catches.

the clutches of
my personal hell
let loose.

i'm set free.

i blink into the sun.
nothing familiar,
yet everything the same.

where have i been?

This poem was inspired by Plato's Allegory of the Cave.

<u>purpose</u>

sandy beach
so rough,
so soft,
once big,
now small.

is that what i am?
am i ground down,
beaten,
torn,
ripped apart,
until i am nothing
but small pieces
of what i once was?

the waves beat
tirelessly.
they wash ashore,
erase my accomplishments,
my struggles
and my existence.

i feel powerless.
my life carried
to places unknown.
yet, i'm still here.
one among many.

we all struggle,
and we all survive.
small pieces
of a big puzzle.
unimaginable,
seemingly impossible,
but accepted.
for we have a purpose
unknown to most of us.
part of a bigger picture
we cannot see,
and maybe never will.

but, when the sun sets,
the result is gorgeous.
a breathtaking view
of what we have become.

looking within

you help me be a better me
from a place within that's hard to see.
though vines of defenses wrap my mind,
you ask the questions of a deeper kind.

"who's this about? it's more than just you."
"maybe this hurt, others are feeling it, too."
"look past the ego and ask yourself: 'why?'"
"look past what you know and see with the eye."

any pain from the past that still sits within
is the first step of awareness and place to begin.
we gain the most when we learn to let go
and allow life to use us and let ourselves grow.

this desire for growth must start from inside
by first facing the hurt that's protected by pride.

i question the narrative of who i am.
an author of perspective, do you understand?
everything i tend to take personally,
but never was, nor will it ever be, just about me.

this action for growth isn't easy to do.
surrendering ego and what we think to be true.
humanity heals when one opens their mind
and asks the questions of a deeper kind.

who's this about? it's more than just you.
maybe this pain, others are feeling it, too.
look past the ego and ask yourself, "why?"
look past what you know and see with the eye.

<u>depth</u>

when i look into the eyes of another
and they really feel that they're seen,
the spirit connection is tangible.
it's a whole new depth of their being.

CHAPTER TWO:

love

<u>turmeric (and black pepper)</u>

you are light in the dark,
a fairy in a normal world,
an artist where art is needed
and a wild flower amidst fields of grass.

you're a healer,
a believer
and a timeless human soul.

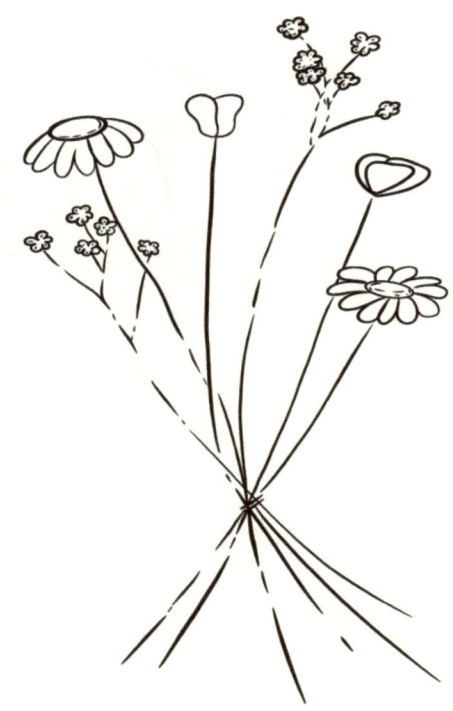

<u>melody</u>

hello baby, can't you see
the fruit growing on that tree?
the contrast beauty
three by three,
art making shapes out of you and me.

<u>for you</u>

a poem for you.
(those words are new)
why have i never devoted love
in a musical way to you?

you offer support,
understanding,
safety and attention.

a part of me wants fire,
mystery and thrill.
a magical feeling down my spine.

when i said, "i love you,"
what did those words even mean?
an empty promise of what i wish
i could give.

your eyes don't hold
the depth that i crave.
i crave meaning,
curiosity,
a pull for more life.

you give me sustainability.

where is the storm?

<u>unfinished dreams</u>

it's not fair to you or to me
to finish a puzzle
that's missing two pieces
or three.
to say it's complete
would be untrue, you see.

who am i to give
incomplete hope
to a dream
that's not new?

do we accept its known faults,
or do we fix it with glue?

<u>meteor</u>

let me blaze as bright as i can
and then

let
me
go.

let me light up your world
and then
fade

to where no one knows.

<u>constellations</u>

you were this beautiful piece of art,
pearl white and mysterious.
a contrast that drew me in.
i had no desire but to have.
not to be had, mind you.

you asked me to stay
under the light of your stars
and to give up the sun of the day.
you held this offering in empty hands,
and your mystery faded
into the night sky
full of mapped out constellations.

now that i've studied your art
and sat under your stars,
i'm not sure that it's what i still want.

what if what's better for me
is still yet to be found?
i can't give up on that.
i can't give up on me.
your beauty will draw others in.
don't ever doubt that your love
is not enough.

it's just not meant for me.

<u>desire</u>

why do i crave the same thing
that makes me a mystery
to myself?

maybe i want a little crazy
because i understand it better.

passion

the power of a firework explosion.
you revolutionize my life
with your eyes.
the slow precision of a king's carver.
vibrant colors shifting vision
to other worlds.

you paint me,
yet you are the art.

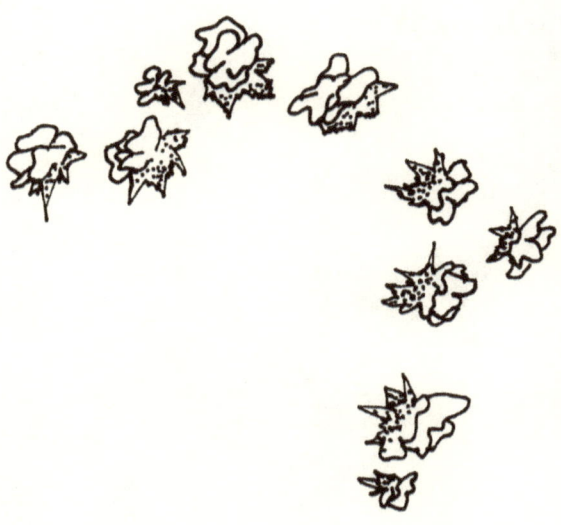

<u>naive</u>

you are me in every way.
i come alive from the ways
in which you see me.
too real to be a dream.

you inspire me in ways that let loose
the need to express this experience.
my vision sees everything
a million ways at once.

will you be mine forever
without being mine?

<u>innerbloom</u>

eyes closed,
the whisper of your soft lips
feed the fire of my heart.
apocalyptic.
my favorite scene on repeat.

time an illusion,
lost to the beats of the moment.
please know,
your eyes hold a depth
that make me believe in a god.

stars explode,
caught by the colors
that your hands bring to life.
is it enough?

enraptured by your existence.
you are the sweetest melody.

i know there must be an end.
my intuition puts salt where i lick.

psychedelic
===

you are a reflection of me,
the parts of ourselves
we don't want to see
but that bring us closer to intimacy.

i know myself better
by learning to love you.
by being loved by you.

my mirror,
my catalyst,
my fire.

<u>roots</u>

sunrise moonset
and breaths of fresh air.
exploratory canvases,
and we are the art.

painting dreams in the sky
with breathtaking views
that illuminate our world.

expanding our awareness
to find deeper understanding
that eclipses judgment form.

watering our hearts,
the roots take shape,
connected by unity above.

love, compassion and faith -
seeds that grow
where intention is sewn.

grounded, you set me free.
i love you
with all that can be.

<u>honeycomb</u>

may love fall from us
like sweet honey,

in each moment,
in raw form.

mess,
sweetness
and all.

<u>basil</u>

nature is your playground.
nature is my holy ground.

<u>drought</u>

i've watered this flower
so many times,
you're the one who's not sure
that you want it.

maybe you don't like wildflowers
like i do.

<u>ash</u>

you won't fight for me.

what is more telling
than indecision
coming from someone
who always takes
what they want?

<u>wanted</u>

i want the security
that comes with being wanted.

you want to be wanted
and to be free.

<u>muse</u>

when did i stop
being enough
for you?

when did you start
looking for art
in another?

<u>denial</u>

please don't leave.

leave.

please don't leave.

<u>hope</u>

distant like the taste of spring
while standing in winter's white glory.
believing, holding onto something
that's not quite there to grasp,
yet depending on it to survive.

people have said,
"nothing's real,
everything's an illusion."

if that is true,
then why do i feel
like i'm about to break
into a million forgotten pieces
if you dare take my hope away?

this is the last piece
holding me together
before reality comes
tumbling down.

standing on this precipice,
i know i might fall.
i close my eyes and pray.

for sanity's sake,
i'll pretend it's okay,

while looking to heaven to help me.

if i fall, i will not survive.
the pain of losing you
will be my end.

please,
please don't take my hope away.

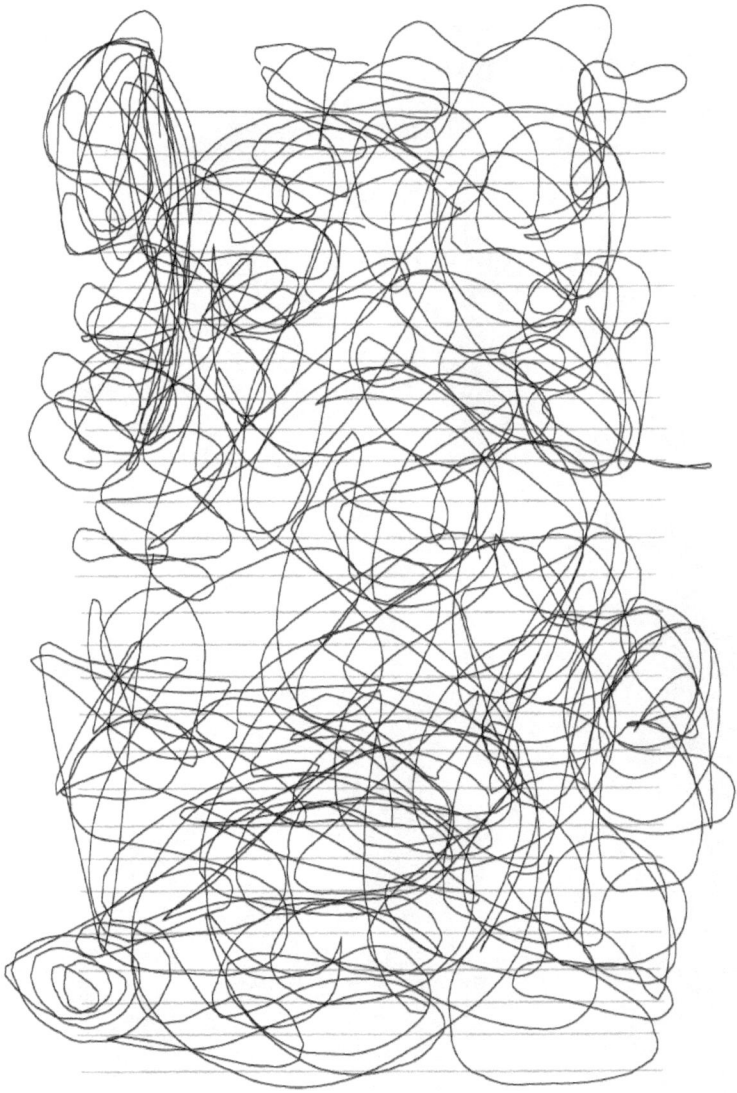

<u>gone</u>

i just want to silence
the emptiness
your absence
left in me.

why won't your memories
let me be?

<u>holding on</u>

if i let you go,
then i make room
for something better.

i've already released
your hold on me
over,
and over
and over again,
and it hurts the same
every time.

why doesn't it hurt you
the way it hurts me?

why am i so attached
to loving you
and to being loved
by you?

preparation

you were my nicotine and
boy, ~~was~~
am i still addicted.

empty space

there is a part of me
that wants you to feel
the hurt
of not having me
since it hurts so much
to not have you.

but, no.

i still want you.

i just want you to want me, too.

<u>3am</u>

i write poems at night
about love,
and i wonder
why i give so much
away.

why do you have
such a hold on me?

why haven't i let you go?

<u>sleepless nights</u>

perennial thoughts
imprison my heart,
reminding her
of a dream
she may never get to hold
again.

<u>on my knees</u>

i feel like i'm at rock bottom.

stuck.
lost.
no place calling me home.

my inner truth says:
"you are exactly where
you are meant to be."

CHAPTER THREE:

healing

<u>time</u>

how is it
that something as sweet
as the smell of fresh rain
still puts salt
on the memories
of when you were here?

why is it
that when the stars
light up the deep, dark night sky,
i still wish
i could share them
with you?

but, you were never
truly mine,
and the stars -
well, they will always shine.

sorrow's river

allowing space to feel
is like releasing a deep river
to flow through spirit, body and soul.

gently cleansing,
it moves the grief
with unapologetic force.

branches torn from shore,
sand unsettled
and stones smoothed over.

timeless.
continuous.

i hold space for this river.
a part of nature
finding its home within me.

<u>surrender</u>

sadness flows like water.
a gentle reminder
of the transience of nature.

<u>one</u>

i am one
with the sounds
of the waves.

nature's company

she looked to the tree beside her
and said, "thank you for being here."

   "i am here," it responded.

she saw a few people down by the shore.

   "you don't validate me like others do," she
noticed out loud.

   "you are here," it replied.
   "i am here," she agreed.

she held its roots tightly
as they looked to the sea,
enjoying each other's company.

<u>healing</u>

a kind process,
held in earth's gentle care.

the forest

wander into my open arms.
explore the earth with bare feet.
connect to the eternal breath
circulating through the trees.

it's okay to not be okay,
just do your best to communicate.
communication -
an expression of the soul;
freedom of the internal.

strength.
vulnerability.
really seeing and being seen.

forgive yourself.
let time heal like a river finds its way.
let your spirit rest,
for everything is temporary.

just as seasons come and go,
the flow of life
is magical.

let this moment take you
wherever you go,
even when it's uncomfortable.

<u>warm embrace</u>

the breeze kisses my arms
and wraps my body,
reminding me i'm alive.

the moon guides my heart
as it softly rests
high in the faded night sky.

<u>rediscovered</u>

may i get lost in my surroundings
to further find myself.

<u>to be</u>

to be still in the sunshine
and to breathe the same air
as the sky and the trees.

it is about listening, not knowing.

<u>we are</u>

i am a tree.
i am the water.
i think, therefore i am.
i breathe, therefore i am.
i am, just as you are.

everything
is temporary

the only constant
is Change.

<u>rebirth</u>

my body finds peace
in the sand's soft bed.
my skin finds solace
in the dance of the waves
as they move in sync
with the tide.

back and over.
over and back.

serenity.

the sun shines.
a source of warmth and all-knowing.
a constant spectacle in the sky.
here i lie.
my loose clothing become one
with the water
as it flows over me
before returning to source.

rebirth.

my body re-energized
in this meditative state.

i am one with the waves.

reminder

i write affirmations
on fallen leaves
and offer them to the water.

every part of who i am
is taken care of.

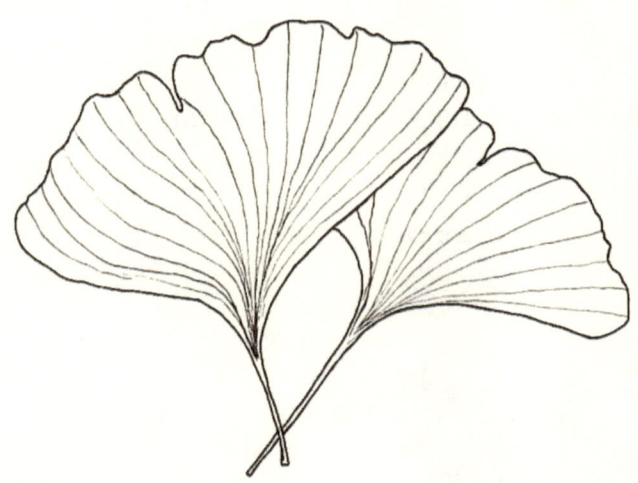

gratitude
_____

eyes closed, i whisper, "thank you."
words sent out to a space
infinite with abundance.

i feel whole without feeling full.
enough without validation.

"thank you."
a message sent out and received.
my spirit gives thanks to the unknown.

i am known in the unknown.
sitting here, i am where i am meant to be.
sweet serenity.

can i take this unknown with me?

<u>internal peace</u>

like rain falling from the river of peace
flowing through heaven's sky of stars.
a natural occurrence of divinity and creation
meeting in dimensions near and one.

a world crafted by daydreams and infinities,
hidden by hopeful illusions
of permanence and mortality.

but dreams never die
and skies never cry,
yet the stars hold maps to our hearts
where that feeling of being seen keeps us alive.

CHAPTER FOUR:

stillness

note from presence

breathe me in.
eclipse judgment form with the sound
of gentle waves crashing in the now.

open your eyes.
experience clarity of what is
by dropping the lens of what should be.

feel my stillness.
notice the weight of expectations released.

be here now.
appreciate my ever-changing impermanence
and unfolding gifts.

let go.
surrender to the flow, unattached,
and breathe in the peace
that expands from within.

<u>free fall</u>

are you present
like the snow?

do you let the moment bring you
wherever it goes?

<u>communion</u>

my authenticity
is born from the stillness
found in communion
with each passing moment.

<u>flow</u>

i've been pushing out
and pulling in
all that i want in my life.

manifestation is easy, right? (no)

surrender to the flow.

<u>downstream</u>

be grounded in uncertainty.

trusting the process
offers peace
when we finally let go.

waterfall

surrender feels like
finally releasing my breath and
letting go
after swimming upstream
against a strong pull.

it feels like
letting myself be swept
into the most peaceful river
crafted by God.

through surrender, i realize
that the waterfall
was all in my head.

acceptance

fear holds tight to the last safe moment,
while desire craves what's next.

acceptance neither grasps nor yearns.
it just is.

<u>freedom</u>

i release the need to have all the answers. i release
the need to have all the answers. i release the need
to have all the answers. i release the need to have
all the answers. i release the need to have all the
answers. i release the need to have all the answers.
i release the need to have all the answers. i release
the need to have all the answers. i release the need
to have all the answers.

<u>be here now</u>

embrace the moment
by surrendering stories of interpretation
constructed by the mind,

then tap into your energy -
the physical energy -
that is felt from being alive.

<u>onism</u>

sitting in meditation, i thought,
"i have nowhere to be."

a soft joy softly bloomed from within
as i surrendered
to the fullness of the moment.

space between thoughts

true creativity comes to us
in the space between thoughts.

when we let go of thoughts,
we drop into the heart,
meeting here
our authentic self.

<u>meditation</u>

take a deep breath
into the stomach.
feel it expand to your back.
savor the fresh air
as it greets your nose
and fills the spaces
of your body.

slowly inhale.
slowly exhale.

look around you.
take in the colors,
the shapes,
the textures.

notice, without judgment,
and then come back
to the breath.

in
and out.
notice some more.

what is it like
to simply *be* where you are?

depth

it's uncomfortable and scary and beautiful
surrendering to stillness,
to the part within that offers
deeper understanding,
love
and acceptance.

there's power
in the awareness
that we are not our thoughts
and our thoughts are not us
and that thoughts
do exist.

there's freedom
in experiencing the tidal wave
of being alive
when all of us
is completely present.

i find myself
the deeper i lose myself,
because the me that exists
is only an image that i think i belong to,
that you think i belong to,
that we think we belong to.

behind everything we think we are,
and everything we think we know,
there is a more beautiful mystery
called the unknown,

found in the stillness
of being.

alive

i am here.
here, right now,
in this timeless moment.

blood pumps through
my vessels.
a soft buzzing energy
vibrates through my body.

i feel grounded
by the sensations
of being alive.

CHAPTER FIVE:

transmutation

<u>invitation</u>

a constant invitation by this moment
of seeking to just be
and breathe
and see
as desires create worlds
under canopies of trees
and next to rivers of surrender
where thoughts of tomorrow
are eclipsed by memories
of the now.

<u>shedding</u>

i shed the layers of who i was,
skin and bone.
unraveling the stale pieces
i'd come to carry as my own.

these parts of me
i've worn for too long,
hindering growth
when it's been time to move along.

i wasn't ready to let them go.

who am i
when i finally surrender;
this old version
of who i used to be?

together

to think this experience
is only mine
would be an illusion.

even my thoughts
are shared in the cosmos.

<u>duality</u>

you are the sweetest melody.
i see you in everything.
i can feel you.

why can't i feel you?

lost in the duality
of my perception
that i am separate,
that this experience
is uniquely my own.
a limiting notion
held in the hands of this body.

"you are what you believe."

i believe in the mystery
of the universe,
in the divine oneness
that weaves us all together.

but, still,
i feel separate, too.

reconnection

spirit, body and soul
meet as one.
this relationship neglected for too long.

so, here i'll return,
over and over again,
to this practice of trusting
the language of my home.

body and being,
together as one.

come home.

<u>sanctuary</u>

hello, body. i feel you.
hello, emotions. i allow you.
hello, mind. i am witness to you.

<u>way of being</u>

happiness feels like
being unattached
to what could be
and fully embracing
what already is.

yet, wisdom whispers:
peace is deeper.

happiness is temporary.
peace
       is a way of being.

mantras (let go)

fear fear fear fear fear fear
release release release release
let go let go let go let go
surrender surrender surrender
be here be here be here be here
believe believe believe

<u>in and out</u>

i inhale gratitude, i exhale fatigue.
i inhale strength, i exhale fear.
i inhale love, i exhale regret.
i inhale the present, i exhale the past.

inhale.
exhale.

<u>breath</u>

thank you.

i have everything i need.

CHAPTER SIX:

flight

lessons

each experience passes through me
as i seek harmony with the wind.

life is about learning,
and we are one.

lessons don't care about time.

<u>loved</u>

i am here.
i am loved.
i am love.

i am here.
i am loved.
i am love.

i am here.
i am loved.
i am love.

i am
here.

i am
loved.

i am
love.

<u>constant</u>

am i who i once was?
surely not,
for i have grown
and matured
through my years.

yet, i still me,
and you are still you.

that stays the same.

<u>timeless</u>

the wise know of time
never ending,
those who can keep
the present moment alive.
forever young,
yet always growing.
one and the same.

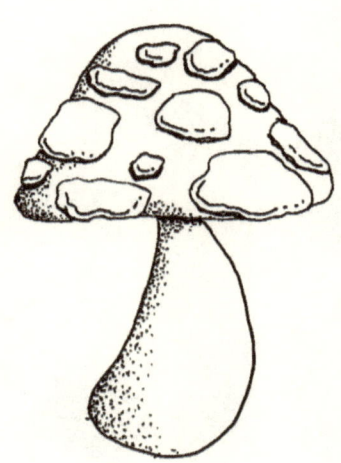

flight

<u>remembrance</u>

remember what truly matters in life.

jungle's insights

1. trust that you are provided for, no matter what.
2. don't waste. use everything to its max.
3. give love even when you don't think you have any left to give.
4. God's love is received when it is shared.
5. you are exactly where you are meant to be.
6. practice regular gratitude.
7. commune with God in each moment.

higher wisdom

hold fast, dear one.
your feet are your roots.
bury them deep in the ground.
connect within
and listen to the song of your heart.

release the chaos echoing from within.
feel the energy of the wind,
the light of the sun,
the support of the earth and
the truth of the trees.

be here now
as the chaos fades away.
focus your attention on love.
ask for serenity.
dress in peace.
undress in freedom.

you are an expression
of the universe.
stay present with knowing.
be free.

<u>letter to self</u>

dear child,
if only you felt
as strong as you are.

never, ever, even for a second,
doubt who you are.
trust those feelings
that are your intuition.

remember you can be
whatever you want.
just believe.

forgive others often,
especially yourself.
laugh easily
and learn to let go.
listen to your body
and honor its needs.

check yourself:
are you acting from a place of love
or of fear?

be true to yourself
even when it feels scary.
be your deepest lover.

let God and others
take care of you.
always move forward
one step at a time.

i love you.

<u>dear friend</u>

let go of the
would haves, should haves
and could haves.
each experience holds a lesson
to be learned.

this moment
invites renewed intentions
with a spirit of forgiveness
and compassion.

always do your best
and let go of regret.
the divine light radiates
whether you open your
eyes to it
or not.

try to be present;
be still.
feel your breath
harmonize with the
symphony of your being.

release attachments
and surrender to change,
to the constant

and inevitable
conductor of life.

relax,
as this moment
will never again
be just as it is
right now.

<u>just listen</u>

believe and trust in yourself
even when you don't think you know.

you always know.

there is never a right
or wrong choice
when it's made with the purest intentions
of love.

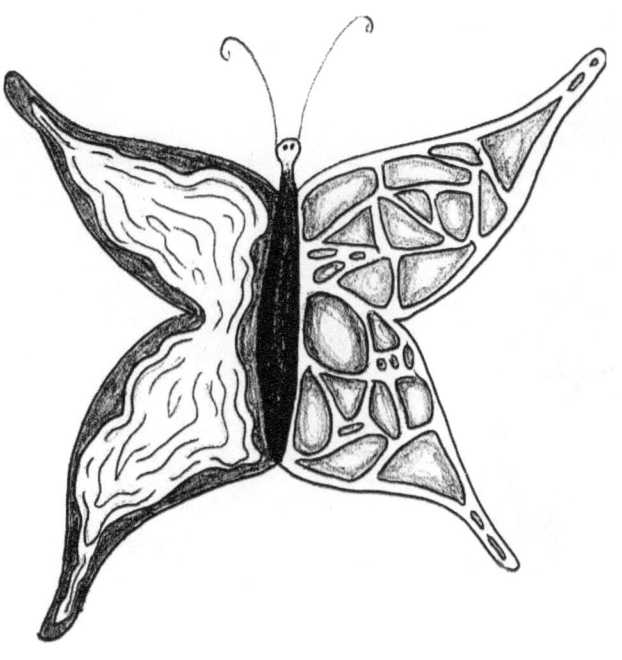

<u>love</u>

respond with love.
breathe with love.
speak with love.
eat with love.
walk with love.
think with love.
see others with love.

respond as love.
breathe as love.
speak as love.
eat as love.
walk as love.
think as love.
see others as love.

be with love.
be as love.

be love.

222

slowly unveiling limiting beliefs
of pretenses and who is right.
cathedral walls standing on thoughts
and built from addicting illusions.
be my sugar, suga.

listen to your intuition.
that gut feeling that says,
"this feels right"
or "maybe i shouldn't."

listen.
create an intimate relationship
with your heart.
be brave with soft edges.
fierce with compassion.

let go to really see.
question the truth.
trust and believe.

shed the layers that hold you back from growth.
find humility through prayer and gratitude.
learn to love yourself unconditionally,
and then love others just as fiercely.

you are exactly where you are meant to be.

midnight sun

create a home
in the sweet abundance of love.
let your young heart dream
of the passions from above.

feel the flow of life
rush through your veins
and the pump of your heart
sing mother earth's name.

reality crafted
through imagination and belief.
deconstruct with the mind.
reconstruct - *do you mind?*

peace in numbers.
peace in no thing.
shine a light,
and free your tethered wings.

dancing in the morning dew,
the flowers bloom by night.

do you?

<u>humility</u>

welcome in the thoughts
that taste like sweetgrass
adorned with dew drop jewels.

the sun smiles upon the mushroom
that bears its cap with humility.

greet discomfort like a childhood friend,
dear to the heart.
presence with gratitude.
surrender by letting go.

come back to the breath.
1, 2, 3, breathe.

unplug to reconnect.
listen to the trees.

<u>harmony</u>

how sweet the reunion
of being one with what is.
a tidal wave of passion
led down-river
in peaceful harmony.

blessed are those
who let themselves go.
who let themselves receive
as they go with the flow.

seek harmony with what is,
and all of the truths
of all of the sages
will come from within.

all of the words
in all the wise books
don't need to be read.
experience them first-hand
by making peace
with the moment.

my tribe

my tribe of sisters
are beautiful and strong.
we sing and we dance
and make art where we go.

fierce, we speak.
brave, we encourage.

we support.
we empower.
we inspire.
we transmute.

connected, there is nothing
we cannot do together.

my tribe sisters, i love you.
let us sing our song
as it is written in the stars.

<u>whole</u>

be you.
bring you.
accept you.

even the part
of you that doesn't
accept you.

accept
and bring that, too.

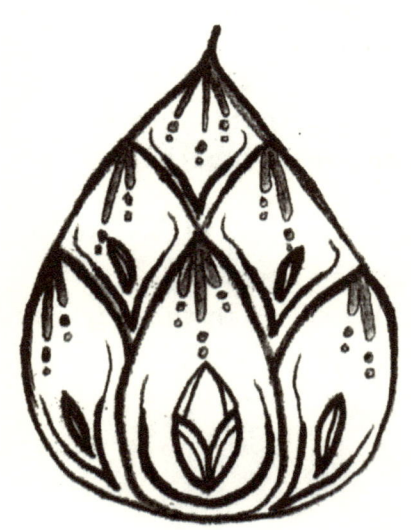

<u>fresh start</u>

crisp air and the crunch of leaves
beneath running feet.
brilliant colors of change
and stunning landscapes.
a beautiful resolution
paving way for new beginnings.

holding hands.
no hands to hold.

this time feels different, though.
last year's lessons
discovering new roots.
the seeds of suffering
finding the light.

same person, new strength.
same name, new power.

i have everything that i need.
no more pitfalls of one more piece
to the perfect scenery.
no more looking for another remedy
to a hole crafted from disillusioned dreams.
this life already a well of abundance.
love from within.
love from above.

i'm untouchable,
yet i touch everything i see.
a trail of love, grace and strength.
forgiveness feeding freedom.
giving more than i take.

a world of abundance.
my own hand to hold.

it's funny,
it was always there.

but, now i see.

<u>nomad</u>

i'm a chameleon that finds safety
no matter where i rest.
my home is in the moment
and under the stars.

<u>phoenix</u>

rising from the ashes on her own two wings,
they told her, "you can't fly."
she remembered a past life where that was true.
but this time, she touched the sky.

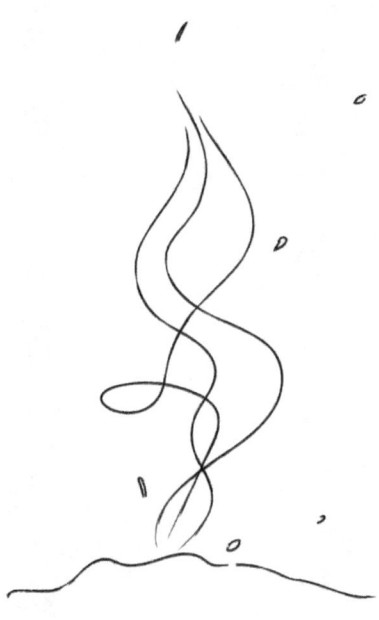

artist recognition

Rachel DiFrancisco
p. 15, 30, 38, 45, 48, 71, 96, 132
racheldifrancisco@gmail.com

Amanda Jacobson
p. 63, 125
amandaccolley@gmail.com

Erin Johnston
p. 27
ejjohnston07@gmail.com

Cassie Kieda
p. 22, 23, 76, 81, 89, 92, 107, 117
instagram: @cassie.kieda.artwork
cassiekieda@gmail.com

Jessica Moog
cover art
jessmoog24@gmail.com

Kristin Wehrum
p. 9
knwehrum@gmail.com

acknowledgments

a cornerstone to the person i am today, i first want to thank my aunt Maria. Maria, you have planted seeds of mindfulness, forgiveness, growth and self-love, over and over again. your inspiration is gently sewn into my life and within the pages of this book.

to my siblings, Rachel, Jenna and Bobby: Rach, you teach me bravery and courage, fashion trends since day one and how success can always go hand-in-hand with having fun. Jenna, you teach me how to laugh, how to accept each moment (and myself) as it is and how to live life deeply and without regret. and Bobby - our adventures together are some of the most meaningful memories i have. you remind me that moments with those we love are the ones that matter the most.

Mom, you teach me unconditional love, and that is the greatest gift of all. i love you. and to the other women in my life who are guideposts to authenticity, i am deeply grateful to know you: Jess, Erin, Whitney, Tina, Katie and Nina, just to name a few. thank you.

acknowledgements

to my tai chi mentors, i hope you know who you are. through your commitment to teaching, i have witnessed and experienced tai chi as a deeply spiritual practice. i aspire to be like you someday.

to everyone else whose name was not mentioned but who has had an impact in my life, thank you. your support and love are what helped get me here. and lastly, thank you to each and every one of my readers, whether we have met yet or not. you, by reading these words, bring them to life.

may we all remember our wings to fly.

to leave a book review or to
connect with the author, visit
www.mindfulnesswithkate.com

www.ingramcontent.com/pod-product-compliance
Lightning Source LLC
Chambersburg PA
CBHW031413120626
46545CB00006B/2126